Dog Heaven and Cat Hell Are Probably the Same Place

(And other ridiculously deep thoughts)

J.J. Harlan

DOG HEAVEN AND CAT HELL
ARE PROBABLY THE SAME PLACE

Written by J.J. Harlan

Photos courtesy of Pixabay.com and Negativespace.com.

ISBN 13: 978-1-961492-02-8 (paperback)

ISBN 13: 978-1-961492-04-2 (hardcover)

Library of Congress Control Number: 2023914205

DEDICATION

To my Uncles Gary and Rob,

If a person's sense of humor is any indication of their health, may the three of us get the professional help we desperately need.

I just read a story about cannibals on a remote island that threw stranded sailors in a big pot and boiled them into soup. That's disgusting! Everybody knows people don't taste good unless they are properly sautéed.

If cats could talk, I bet that when they cleaned themselves they'd never shut up about how good they taste.

Whenever you bring the word "milk" up in conversation, make sure you pause and clarify it's not "breastmilk" that you're talking about. Otherwise, people might be weirded out.

I think it would be a good idea if scientists invented a new fruit. It should look like an orange, but "surprise," it tastes like a watermelon. Also, it screams when you peel it.

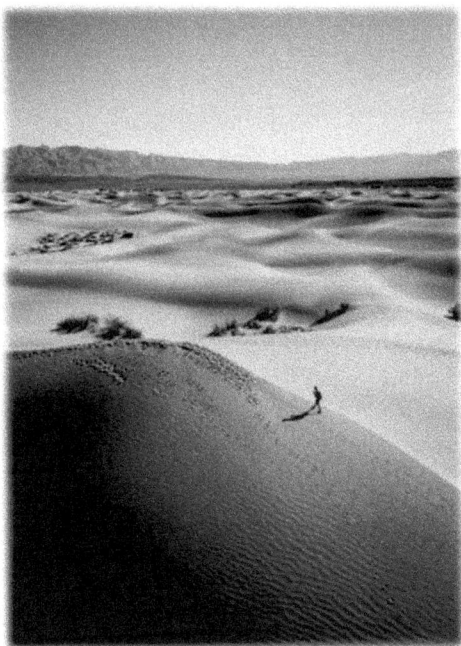

Here's a tip if you ever get stuck in quicksand: don't struggle, you'll just sink faster. Instead, repeatedly clench your buttocks as quickly as possible to propel yourself up and out of the quicksand.

If you ever spend the night in a haunted mansion, be careful when you use the bathroom. That's where the pervert ghosts like to hang out.

As I drove the locomotive full speed through the beautiful countryside, I tooted the train whistle and realized this might be the greatest day of my life.

Probably not so much for the conductor banging on the door, begging to be let back into the engine room.

If Martians landed in downtown New York, I'm sure they'd be surprised at the number of hot dog stands in the city. You just don't find that many on Mars.

What is true love? It's hearing your lover tell you the same boring story you've already heard a thousand times and not stabbing them in the eye.

I bet when aliens abduct people to perform experiments on them, they probably make them sign a bunch of waivers first.
An intergalactic malpractice suit could get pretty complicated.

Many people don't realize that "The Man" is actually a fellow by the name of Jasper Hammond who runs a convenience store in Iosha, Wisconsin.

If you ever catch a fish, and it just so happens to be a magic fish that will grant you any three wishes if you throw him back in the water, don't do it! Those talking fish are good eating.

If I wore a glass eye, and I was on a really boring dinner date, I think popping it out and performing sleight-of-hand magic tricks with it could be a great way to liven up the evening.

Can you imagine what it must've been like for the last dinosaur that ever lived? I'm sure part of him was lonely, but there was also that part of him that was glad there were no more long lines for the bathrooms.

It'd be a great idea to have firefighters wear holsters and carry guns like the police do. Of course, they wouldn't be real guns, just water pistols.

I bet that dog heaven and cat hell are probably the same place.

Probably in the olden days, peasants who didn't have money for spices like salt or pepper seasoned their food with sand instead. It was tough times for those peasants.

I think the Olympics should include more sports that involve gardening or sewing.

It boggles my mind how often people are rude in elevators. Every single time I press all the buttons at once, people get upset. C'mon folks, take the stairs if you're in such a hurry.

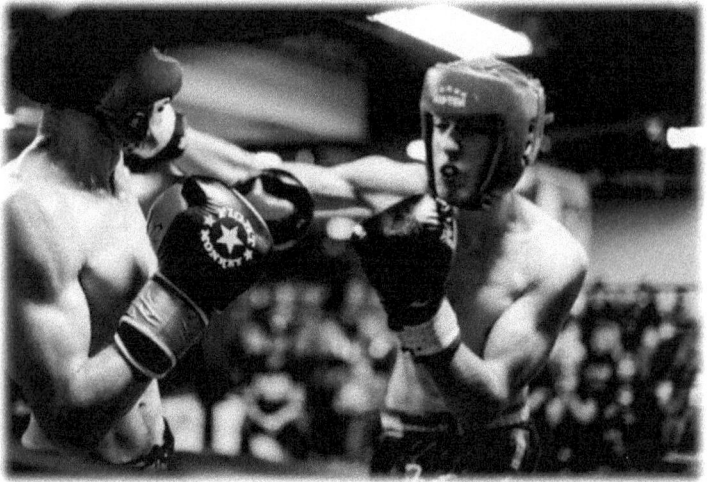

Two good tips for boxers in a boxing match are: don't let your guard down, and always taunt your opponent in rhyme.

If you could go back in time and talk to the ancient Egyptians about modern life, I think it'd be the invention of the Cheeto that would fascinate them the most.

I once read a book that stated there are more insects living on the planet than people. Neat fact.

It didn't specify which planet, so I can't speak to that.

There are two types of people in this world: those that enjoy eating in the nude, and those that kick you out of the restaurant when you're trying to do just that.

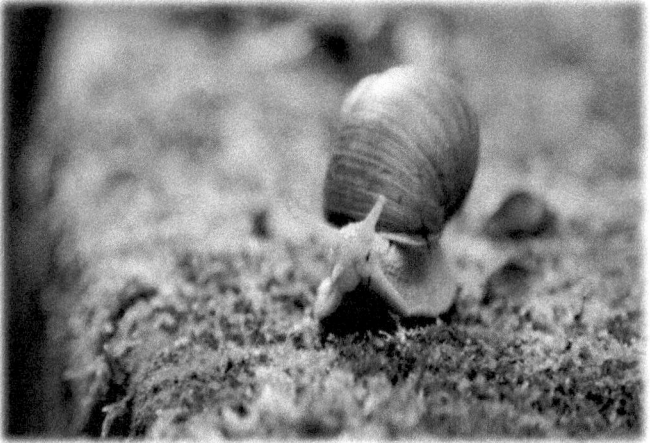

In many ways, the snail is the wisest of creatures. "Why?" you ask. If you were a snail, you would already know.

Everyone's impressed when my two-year-old nephew points to the sky and says "bird," but when I do it, they just stare at me. You people are impossible to please!

I bet when the movie "Rocky" premiered, a lot of angry geologists demanded refunds in theaters.

If you work as a Santa in the mall during Christmastime, and you're drunk, and you throw up on a kid sitting in your lap, I think you should tell him it was probably the milk and cookies he gave you last year.

The Romans are remembered for their great contributions to the civilized world: mainly, paved roads, aqueducts, and the first Wal-Mart.

I asked Rebecca if she knew what clouds tasted like and she said they don't taste like anything, they're just made up of large collections of tiny ice crystals suspended in the atmosphere.

Hahaha, sure honey. It's okay to admit you just don't know.

When you think about it, fishing is nothing more than a tug of war contest using a tiny rope.

I think a good idea for a movie would be about a little boy learning to play the fiddle. All the other children laugh and tease him for taking fiddle lessons. Then, one day, his mother pulls an old dusty fiddle out of the attic and says, "This was your grandfather's magic fiddle. Whoever plays this fiddle will be the world's best fiddler." Then, all the other children will feel real bad about making fun of the little boy because now he was the world's best fiddler.

Man, I hated those stupid fiddle lessons.

Calligraphy is a lost art nowadays. Also, sneezing with one's eyes open.

Old people can easily be compared to an old book. On the outside, they might look plain and boring, but when you take the time and look inside them, you probably learn a lot of things you never knew. Things you don't care about and that are pretty boring. Instead of wasting your time with the "book," you probably want to watch TV or something.

If you're making a cake, and the recipe ever calls for a cup of "milk," it's most likely referring to cow's milk. Trust me on this one.

If I could be any animal, I'd be a bird. You might think it's because they can fly, but that's not the reason. It's because nobody looks at them funny when they're eating worms.

One way you can find out the time of day is to use the sun. If you stare at it long enough, you won't be able to see anymore. As you stumble around, bumping into things because you're blind now, someone may come and offer you help. When they do, ask them if they know what time it is.

I'm sure the first maps were nothing more than a paper with squiggly dotted lines and a "You are here" written on it.

If you ever find yourself hard at work building a diabolical giant robot to take over the world, make sure you take breaks and get some fresh air now and then so as not to burn yourself out.

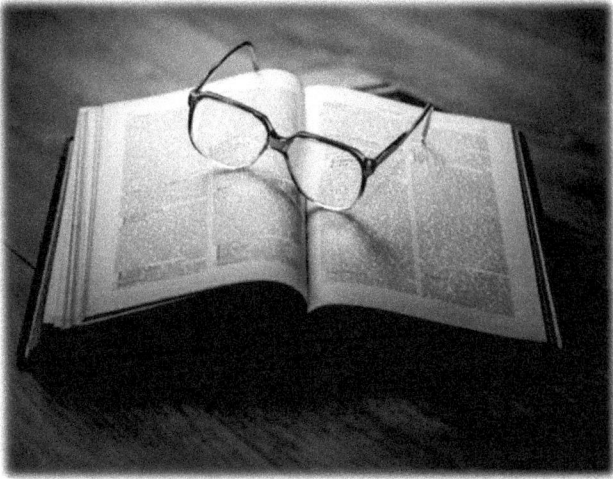

The best kind of book is one that's written about a character with a problem, who then rises to meet the challenge, and finally overcomes it in the end. Also, it has a scratch-and-sniff page that smells like pizza at the back.

A good life tip is to bring a stick of butter with you to bed every night. That way if you wake up during the night and want some butter... BAM! It's right there!

The saddest thing in the whole world is a crying clown who realizes that the humongous shoes he's wearing are actually the real size of his feet.

What is the smartest animal in the world?

If you said, "a dolphin," you'd be wrong. It's a chicken with its medical degree. Surprised? You shouldn't be. Medical school is hard.

As a kid I loved going to Sunday school. I still remember my favorite stories about Jesus walking on water, feeding the crowds with fishes and loaves, and shooting laser beams out of his eyes.

Nothing says "I love you" like a homemade handwritten card slipped under your lover's pillow while they're sleeping... despite that ridiculous restraining order.

Give a man a fish, and he eats for a day. Teach a man to fish, and he becomes lazy and skips work to do it.

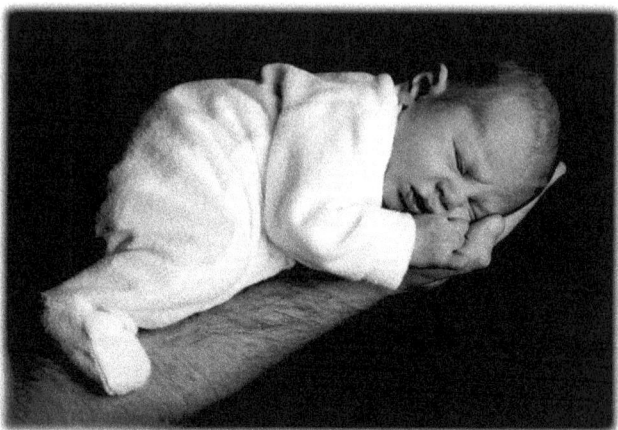

When I have my first kid I will call him "A". I'll name all my other children after a different letter of the alphabet. When "Z" is born, we'll stop having kids, because then I'd have to name them after numbers. Only a weirdo would name their child after a number.

There is only one thing faster than the speed of light, and that is the run to the bathroom after two chili cheese dogs and Crazy Carl's Coaster.

You'll never find a meteorite made out of cheese, and you know why? Cheese burns up too easily as it falls through our atmosphere.

People just can't seem to take compliments anymore. Like the lady I complimented at the grocery store pushing a baby stroller with a cute monkey in it.

Nothing tastes sweeter than biting into ripe summer strawberries. Also, licking the handlebar of the mechanical car ride at Chuck E. Cheese.

The three most challenging moves to master in Kung-Fu are "The Dancing Tiger," "The Hidden Dragon," and "The Barking Chihuahua."

Rebecca says I should take up a hobby. Uh, excuse me? What do you think I'm doing hiding in the bushes waiting for people to walk by?

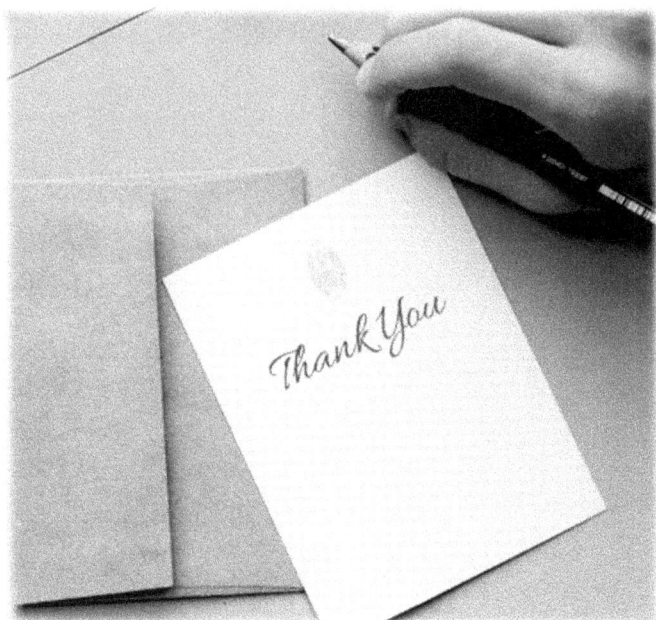

Let's face it, burglars who leave behind thank-you notes are the most well-mannered and polite of criminals.

I think it would be neat to be a Marine and let me tell you why. You wear a cool uniform, learn to drive a tank, and get to ring a bell while collecting change in a red bucket at Christmastime.

How much wood could a woodchuck chuck if a woodchuck had a chainsaw?

I bet a popular joke in medieval days was to sneak up behind a knight and stick a "kick me" sign on his armor with a magnet.

Whenever you go to a restaurant and have to wait for a table, tell the hostess your name is "Parpar." That way, when it's your turn, they'll call out: "The Par-par-party table is ready."

I think fortune cookies should be more realistic with their fortunes. "You shouldn't have eaten the cashew chicken," or "Your spouse is cheating on you," are probably accurate predictions for some of the people out there.

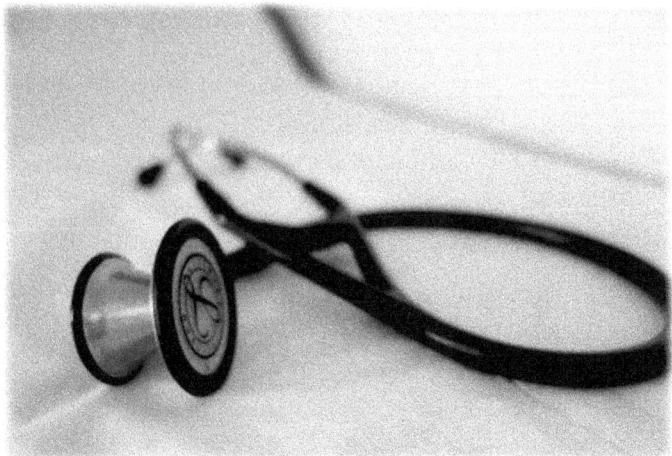

If I were a nurse about to give a patient a shot, I think it'd be a funny joke to squirt a little bit into your mouth first and say, "Yup, it's not the poison!," then stick it into the patient real fast.

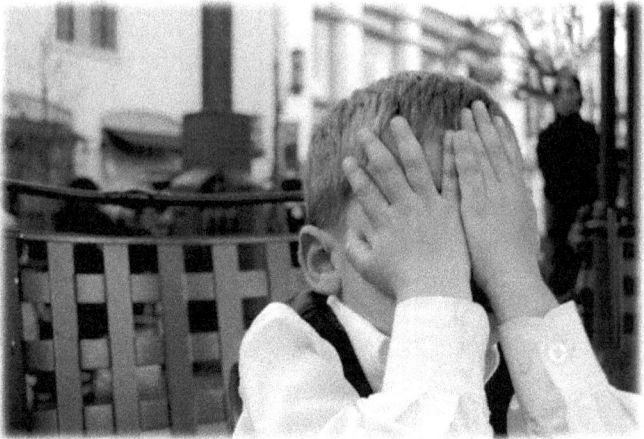

For kid vampires, pretty much the most embarrassing thing in the world is when all your friends already have their adult fangs, but you still have your baby nubbins. Hang in there little buddy, they'll come in one day.

If you throw a boomerang, and it doesn't come back to you, it was probably just a stick, so, no big loss.

I read somewhere that man is descended from monkeys. I don't know if it's true, but it would explain a lot, especially about my Uncle Roger.

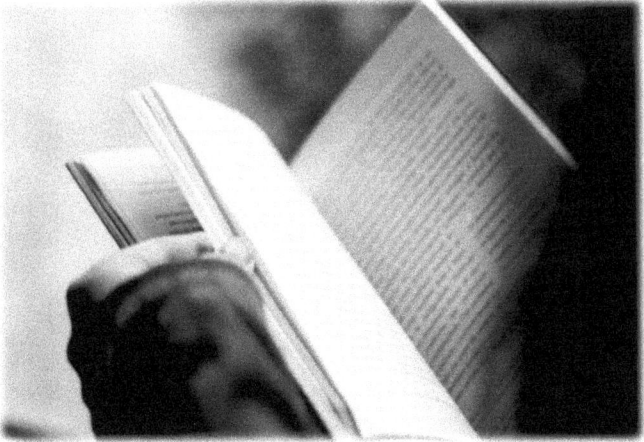

I don't think kidnappers should offer candy and toys to kids. They should offer something educational, like a calculator or a good book. Kids don't read enough nowadays.

When you're a little kid and something traumatic happens, it sticks with you for the rest of your life. For instance, I'll never forget the time my mom robbed a bank. We walked in, went straight to the teller, and she said, "I want some money." The teller told her to fill out some slips and sign them. Then my mom pulled out her checkbook and wrote some stuff down then we waited as the teller counted it out. Then my mom walked out with the money. It's sad when children are exposed to criminal behavior like that.

I bet when a racehorse is done running a really hard race, it probably thinks to itself, "Yeah, it's Miller time." And then it's disappointed when all it gets is a carrot or an apple.

L aundry tip: If you wear
your underwear on the
outside of your pants,
you can go twice as long
without having to wash them.

We never see police using drug-sniffing pandas, probably because they're more susceptible to addiction problems.

I remember the time a Bigfoot ate our mailman. Luckily, my Uncle Roger and I caught the Bigfoot with a bear trap in our front yard before he could escape. The Bigfoot had put on our mailman's clothes and even stole his mailbag. He was screaming stuff like, "Let me go!" and "I am the mailman, you idiots!" Yep, some people called Uncle Roger crazy, but I called him a hero.

If I had a nickel for every time a child laughed, I'd probably try real hard to invent some sort of laugh-o-matic machine to use on them so I could get rich.

Lying on my back while looking up at the stars, I realize what a magnificent universe we live in. It's huge. It's inspiring. Also, I'm pretty drunk right now and can't stand up.

I'm sure if you could understand spider language, you'd hear nothing but filthy swearing every time you walked into one of their webs.

I used to love watching that show "The Muppets" with Kermit the Frog. Many people don't realize how many years it took to train those animals to talk.

Isn't it funny to think about how some things began? Like, the first "bank" was probably just some guy who said to his friend, "Hey, I've got an idea. Give me all your money, and whenever you want some, you can ask me for it."

If little boys are made of snips and snails, and little girls are made of sugar and spice, then what are leprechauns made of?

ABOUT THE AUTHOR

J.J. Harlan is a humorist and science fiction writer located in the magical, mystical land of the Pacific Northwest. When he's not drinking coffee and dreaming up strange worlds, he's hiking in the mountains with his wife, ever on the lookout for a UFO or a friendly Bigfoot.

Please check out J.J. Harlan's other books: *Aliens and Androids* and *How Not to Be Helpful: An Illustrated Guide for Thoughtless Adults* available at Amazon and fine bookstores everywhere.

www.ingramcontent.com/pod-product-compliance
Lightning Source LLC
Chambersburg PA
CBHW052120030426
42335CB00025B/3068